Empty arms

Empty arms

A mother's journey

through grief to hope

Keren Baker

PUBLISHING WITH A MISSION

EP BOOKS

Faverdale North, Darlington, DL3 0PH, England

e-mail: sales@epbooks.org

EP BOOKS

P. O. Box 614, Carlisle, PA 17013, USA

e-mail: usa.sales@epbooks.org

web: http://www.epbooks.org

First published 2009

British Library Cataloguing in Publication Data available

ISBN-13   978-0-85234-704-1   ISBN 0-85234-704-9

Printed and Bound in Great Britain by the MPG Books Group

This book is dedicated to my ordinary,
yet beautiful family.
I would be less of a person
without your impact on me.

I also dedicate this book to the
countless number of people who prayed for us.
Most of them we may never meet,
but their prayers helped to sustain us.

Thank you.

Acknowledgements

It has been said by several authors that writing a book can be likened to having a baby. This book has been a very long 'labour' of love! There have been times of pain and frustration as I struggled to write about the grief within my heart, and of my God who has helped me bear it. *Empty arms* has taken much longer than the nine months of human expectancy and would never have been published without the help and support of the following people.

My first thanks must go to all at EP Books and in particular Roger Fay and John Rubens who were instrumental in the publication of this book. They have dealt very patiently with me as we have worked through many things together. Thanks also to David Woollin and his team, Pete Cooper and Jackie Friston, who have worked so hard to produce the manuscript into this final version.

There have been so many other people who have helped with advice about revisions and given useful pointers. These include Jonathan Carswell who really helped shape the initial manuscript and his Dad, Roger, who gave great counsel along the way. I am very grateful to Francis Gleeson who was so perceptive in helping to restructure the book, and to Faith Cook who helped me to have the courage of my convictions. I'm really thankful to Gerard Chrispin whose brain I have 'picked' and advice I have heeded on many occasions! I owe a great debt to Brian, Julie and Norma from Alder Hey. I have learned much about grieving from them and they have been so encouraging with regards to getting the book published.

There are two particular friends whom I must mention: first, Abi, without whose friendship and her suggestion of trying to get the manuscript published, this book would not exist now; and second, Gill, who has been such a support in encouraging me to keep going during the publishing process; I owe her much. 'Thank you' to both these amazing women. I also appreciate Sarah James, for giving of herself, her time and her photography skills.

I cannot forget my parents; they have listened to my 'ups' and 'downs' during the time of working on this book and have been so patient despite not yet having read it. They have been grieving alongside us and have still given unwavering support.

Lastly I must thank Steve, the man who has put up with me for over fifteen years. He has stood by me and supported me at times when he has hardly felt able to deal with his own emotions, let alone mine. He has enabled me to find time to do revisions and has encouraged me to continue working on *Empty arms* when I felt like giving up.

I trust that this book will be a comfort to those that need comforting. I also hope it might be a reminder to others that our days are numbered. Writing this book has helped me to remember that we need (with God's help) to make our short lives count for eternity and to bring glory to the God who loves us.

Contents

Foreword

It is hard to imagine any greater pain than that of losing a little child. It is like an amputation, so that though one may learn to live with the loss, the parent is never the same again. In the English language we have a word for those who have lost their parents: an orphan. We have a word for those who have lost their spouse: a widow or widower. We have no word for those who have lost a child. It is as if the very thought is too painful to put into words. Steve and Keren Baker had been committed Christians for several years before the uninvited intruder of death broke into their lives. Snatched from them was a gorgeous two-year-old, Nattie, who had a twin brother. Within the space of just one morning their lives were to be turned around.

I have no doubt that to write an account of how she coped and even had peace in the midst of her loss was truly therapeutic for Keren. Through the immense hurt that the family has endured she has given us a thoroughly honest account of the peaks and troughs of bereavement. For Keren, the loss she has experienced has brought refinement from life's dross, as produced within her has been the gold of deeper understanding, faith, trust and compassion. What has happened has not made Keren bitter, but better.

God never wastes any tears nor pain. All that Keren has endured, little Nattie has been spared, and all that one day will be Keren's eternally is Nattie's now. Nattie is with Christ, which is far better. These are not just the glib or garbled words of someone trying to give comfort to grieving parents, but are the bedrock of the confidence that the parents have for their little girl.

Empty arms is an intensely practical book which has as its basis the autobiographical experience of a lovely family ravaged by death. Everyone would benefit from reading and understanding about bereavement, but for anyone in a similar situation to the Bakers, this account is not only a text book but a tonic, and may even be a true friend.

Roger Carswell

Introduction

You shouldn't outlive your children. It's not the correct order of life. It's not natural to survive beyond them when your prime parental instinct is to ensure their survival. However, 'survive', ironically, seems to be the key word. I am surviving.

Some days my head barely feels above water. People may think I'm managing fairly well but, beneath the surface, my feet are paddling furiously to keep me afloat. Other days, I feel more able to cope. I would not say that I have triumphed over grief; it is more a case of 'getting through'.

This book is about my journey through grief, a journey that is still continuing. It isn't a text book on the best way to grieve — in any case, I believe every path through suffering is unique. Nor is this a 'how to' book giving clichéd advice. It is simply a collection of lessons learnt, some of which have been forged indelibly on my heart in the furnace of bereavement. Partly, it is a personal, cathartic record of the long and slow path we are forced along once a loved one dies. Mostly, it is a journey of faith.

Whatever your current situation may be, I hope that this book encourages you. I do not write as an expert as I'm still fumbling my way through. Some of these pages are just a snapshot of the early weeks of our loss and how we struggled to face this new chapter in our lives, upheld so tangibly by God, whose mercies really are 'new every morning'. Although I have faith, I struggle as much as anyone. What keeps me going is the knowledge that my toughest days are *never* beyond the reach of his care or faithful love. He knows every time I feel that my heart is breaking and he does not remain unmoved or dispassionate. The God who watched his only Son die alone understands how alone you may feel too.

I know there will be many more valleys to cross and plenty of dark days ahead. But they will never be completely dark, because God is my light; and the valleys will never completely engulf me because he has promised that I will never be forsaken. On this earth, the way ahead is uncertain, but heaven is always closer than it was yesterday, and our hope is sure and certain even if the journey is not. My loss here on earth is heaven's gain, and I *will* see my little girl again. However, even though we long to see her, heaven will be much more than just a reunion. Heaven is him. When I see God face to face, all my struggles will have been worth it. For on that day my arms will no longer be empty, and his arms will be around us all in our eternal home, where there are no more tears and no more suffering.

1.
Nattie

Some dates are etched into the memory for ever. For some, it's a wedding or a birth, a first job, or the day they moved into their first house. For me, 10 May 2006 is the date that marks the 'before' and 'after' of my life. Just as Christ's birth marks the beginning of the new era of AD after BC, so this date marks the beginning of a new chapter for my family.

We were a very ordinary couple, our lives possibly busier than most, with the usual chaos and joys of raising a young family of five children. As newly-weds, Steve and I never deliberately planned a large family as we saw having children very much as a gift from God, but we delighted in being able to love and care for each one. We had been blessed with Suzannah (then aged nine), Heather (seven), Harriet (three) and Jamie and Natalie, our two-year-old twins. Our lives were immersed in work, church and family, and everything seemed fine. It hadn't always been so. We had been through a few difficult years with miscarriages, illness and unemployment, but the Lord had helped us through and, at long last, things seemed to be starting to settle down a little. It's as well we cannot see into the future as we could not have coped with knowing what was about to shake our world.

The day before Nat died was unremarkable in its entirety. I had done the school run to a wonderful school the older girls had moved to the previous September. I then travelled on to the local supermarket to pick up a cake to share with the other children at Toddler Group as it was Harriet's birthday that Thursday. Harriet chose the cake and we all carried the items to the checkout. I remember people smiling at my little trio as they meandered down the aisles. I was so proud of my children, and having twins attracted many comments (mostly positive!).

At Toddler Group the morning passed quickly as usual; although Natalie was very clingy. She didn't really participate, not even during the craft activity, which she normally loved.

We arrived back home and I put all the children down for their nap. I heard Nattie wake earlier than expected and found that she had been sick. This was nothing unusual. As parents of young children, we were used to the usual round of sickness bugs that tended to be caught from school, first by the older girls, then passed on to the rest of the family. So I cleaned Nattie up and laid her on the sofa with a blanket. She lay there for the afternoon with a fan to keep her cool and paracetamol to keep her temperature down. Later, I had to take her out to pick up the girls from school, but when we arrived back home she was pretty exhausted and remained like that for the rest of the day. We were still not unduly concerned: our children had been ill with temperatures before, and had appeared more poorly on previous occasions than Nattie did then.

After tea, I went out to a women's Bible study and Steve looked after the children. While I was out, Nattie had asked to go to bed and was asleep when I returned, but I woke her to give her more medicine. Still there was nothing that gave us particular concern. Steve checked her before we went to bed, as he did every night for all of our children, and she was sleeping soundly.

It was during the early morning rush the next day that one of the children came in to tell us that Nattie did not want to get out of bed. My older girls liked to run into the twins' room every morning and lift them out of their cots, then all of them would run into our bedroom, and thus our joyfully hectic mornings would begin. However, this day was different. When one of the girls tried to lift her out, she'd said, 'No.' Steve quickly went to her and brought her into our bedroom; it was obvious she was in a very poorly state. As an experienced mum, I do not usually panic over the children, but as soon as I saw her, alarm bells rang inside me.

We immediately called the ambulance. I held her and talked to her while we waited impatiently for it to arrive. Her breathing was really laboured. We know now that she was dying even then. I held her hand in the ambulance as it rushed her to hospital. She arrived there alive, but the infection was simply overwhelming her despite everyone's best efforts to prevent it.

Nattie had contracted a rare bacterial disease called *Haemophilus Influenza type B*. Ironically, she had been vaccinated against it as a baby. Her immunisation had evidently not been entirely successful at providing protection, and that, coupled with the fact that this bacteria was particularly aggressive, meant that Natalie simply could not fight off the disease. She succumbed to its very virulent strain and her death was swift and almost inevitable. She had been in the Emergency Department of the hospital for less than forty-five minutes when they told me that she had died.

And so, our world fell apart.

2.
Early days:
coping one day at a time

To be honest, at the beginning, a day felt like an eternity — simply getting through the next hour seemed enough of an achievement. As the enormity of what had happened sank in, the days, weeks and months to come seemed unendurable. Looking ahead completely overwhelmed me. I couldn't cope.

Then I recalled the words of Jesus, 'Therefore do not worry about tomorrow, for tomorrow will worry about its own things. Sufficient for the day is its own trouble,' (Matthew 6:34), and they hit home with fresh force. My focus had to be on the *now*, not the future, and definitely not the past. I knew that I had to take one step at a time, looking to God for my strength as I was bereft of any of my own. Christians often try to memorize verses from the Bible so that they are inscribed on our hearts. Again and again, verses from the Bible that I had learnt previously, as well as words of choruses, would pop into my head, offering me comfort just at the moment I needed it. The words of Jesus came to me: 'Come to Me, all you who labour and are heavy laden, and I will give you rest. Take My yoke upon you and learn from Me, for I am gentle and lowly in heart, and you will find rest for your souls. For My yoke is easy and My burden is light' (Matthew 11:28-30). These words provided me with such relief! I realized I did not have to bear this crushing burden on my own due to the simple fact that I wasn't alone.

Many of you will have read the famous poem called 'Footprints'. For those of you who do not know it, it is a poem about someone who looks back on his life as though it is a walk by the sea. Throughout all the different phases of his life, he can see the marks of his footprints, and those of Jesus who walks with him. What perplexes him is that, when he follows the trail left behind through the bad times, there is only one set of prints; whereas through the good times, there are two. Times of great grief and hardship can be so bleak that we can feel abandoned by God and the world. The man asks Jesus why he left him to cope alone during those times when he needed him most. And Jesus replies that he did not leave him. He says that, while it is true there is only one set of prints through those times, it is not because the man was alone, but because he was carried; they are Jesus's footprints.

This poem was especially true of my life. To be fair, I had had a relatively pain-free life up to this point. My childhood was a happy one but something crucial had occurred when I was younger that was to impact my entire life and certainly would make a big difference in dealing with Natalie's death. I had grown up regularly attending the local church where we lived. I had realized fairly early on that I wasn't perfect, and through reading the Bible and hearing God's Word explained to me I soon recognized that I needed to have my wrongdoing dealt with. One night I asked God to forgive me for all the wrong that I had done. I prayed and thanked Jesus for dying for my sin so that I could have forgiveness from God. I knew that by trusting in him

I could know assurance of my wrongs being cleansed and of having a place in heaven when I died. All of this was nothing to do with any good I had done, it was amazingly a completely free and undeserved gift of grace from God. This step of trusting in Christ was to shape my life dramatically as it impacted on every decision that I made. Even marrying Steve was mostly governed by the fact that I wanted to commit my life to someone who shared the same goals, and who loved and wanted to spend his life serving God.

Over the years, when difficulties had entered our lives we had time and again learned to look to the one who had saved us, loved us and wanted the best for us. Being a Christian wasn't easy but was infinitely better than living our lives without knowing God in a real way.

When I look back at those early, harrowing days following Nattie's death, I see the truth of that 'Footprints' poem: how Jesus bore us and comforted our weary hearts. We thought we couldn't bear the pain, but we'll never understand how much more unbearable it would have been without him. We really were carried; I see that now.

So, amazingly, we coped. You just do. You simply have to. *How* you cope is another matter entirely. There are no rules about bereavement, thank goodness. We ought not to worry about what others think. Most people are sensitive enough to understand that each of us has to find our own way through and they do not judge how we find that way. For me, one breakthrough came when I realized that there is no reason why the process of bereavement has to be unrelentingly grim. Despite there being few really great moments, we knew instinctively that it was important to tell our children that it was fine to act normally and it was definitely acceptable to laugh, smile and feel happy, so I had to take this advice myself. I was worried about laughing or smiling in case people thought that I was a bad mother for not being sorrowful enough, but it's important to just accept that your emotions are so raw they are inevitably going to be inconsistent and confused.

One of the most helpful pieces of advice I received about coping was from someone from the Bereavement Team at the hospital. She likened our situation to a piece of blank paper. She explained that, right then, all the emotions we were experiencing, such as pain, distress, anger, sadness etc. were on the left-hand side of the paper. On the right-hand side of the paper were the tasks we had to cope with, such as having to cook a meal, or taking one of the children to the toilet. She told us that, initially, we would spend most of our waking hours experiencing the left-sided emotions. We would have brief intervals where necessary activities would halt our emotions as we concentrated on carrying out these tasks. She explained that we would 'yo-yo' between the two sides of paper constantly, but eventually, the balance would gradually change from the left to the right. We would still return to the left side of the page, but the times spent immersed in these emotions would lessen. How wise, and so incredibly simple and comforting this advice was.

Although her advice was to us as parents, I didn't realize that her insightful explanations had also been taken on board by my seven-year-old until one night in that first week, when I was putting the children to bed, she started to cry and ask me questions. 'Mummy, is it okay to be angry?' she asked. 'Yes,' I said, 'it's fine.' 'But am I allowed to be cross with God?' she continued. I paused to think, then replied, 'Yes, God is big enough to take it, and he understands completely how you feel.' She looked at me and then sighed, 'It's just that I'm on the left side of the page at the moment.'

She was coping, like any child, the only way she knew how. They all did. Some of our children coped best by keeping everything the same, while some were just too young and struggled to grasp what had happened. We anguished about how, as parents, we could best steer our children through this time. Were there things we should not say? Was there a way of behaviour that would make their path through grief ultimately less damaging in the long run? I read many books, but found few answers specifically relating to our situation. So I went back to the best book of all, the Bible. I put my trust in God, knowing that he who made me, loved me and knew me inside out would give me and my family the grace and wisdom so that we could fumble our way forwards and find ways of coping. The first step was to be honest and transparent with our emotions and to trust in God.

Coping was particularly tough when there were no immediate solutions in sight. One of the most distressing things was seeing my youngest son's reaction to bereavement. He had lost his twin, and, not having a twin myself, that was something I could not fully appreciate from his perspective. Having been practically inseparable from birth, his loss must have felt unbearable, and, at two years old, he had neither the comprehension nor the language to express himself. When he was under strain, the depths of his misery were plain to see to everyone.

To begin with, he was confused and extremely unsettled. He would say, 'Nattie in heaven', but at two, heaven was too much of an abstract concept for him, and you could see the confusion in his face. A week or two later, his grief developed into rages. They would often appear out of the blue. Watching him lose himself in regular outbursts was distressing in the extreme.

His rages were quite unlike the toddler tantrums we had seen plenty of times when our other children were that age. It was grief, the outworking of his inner pain. Nothing we did seemed to make any difference to him at the time. We tried holding him, but that had no effect, neither did giving him the space to thrash it out, nor being kind but firm, nor talking him through it.

You name it, we tried it. We felt completely powerless watching as his grief unfolded. How it pained us to stand by and not be able to help him; but he had no other way of expressing it. Two-year-olds don't cry as an emotional release, so what he felt was rage. He didn't have the vocabulary to tell us about his loss and his hurting heart.

When these rages happened in public places, some onlookers were disapproving, their disgusted stares saying it all. I wanted to hang a sign around his neck to make them understand he had just lost his sister, but as they continued with their self-righteous looks I just had to watch and wait and, basically, simply love him.

When he raged, his quaking body would shake until finally he was exhausted and there was nothing left. When he stopped, we would tell him we knew he felt sad, and then we tried to keep things normal for him by carrying on with whatever we had been doing before.

People prayed, we prayed, but again and again he raged; and all we could do was wait. Eventually I realized God was telling me that, hard as it was, I had to stand back and let him grieve. You expect to let go of your children when they are older, but to some extent I had to do it now, as this was something only he could get through, in his own way and in his own time. I wanted to take away all his hurt and pain, but it wasn't just down to me any more. I had to trust God to minister to his little heart and help him to cope.

Even now, as I write this many months later, coping still seems an uphill struggle. Just recently, for example, a difficult family situation that echoed what had happened to us brought the pain and memories flooding back, and the tears came again. The feeling of desperation returned and grief overwhelmed me once more. Over time, the ways of coping seem to change, but the sorrow is ever present and sometimes just as raw.

The key this time for me was finding some music I had not listened to for a while and singing along with it through my tears. As I strode up and down my kitchen, my heart shouted that I could not cope, but my mind was sifting through the truth of what I was singing. With a steely determination matched only by the strength of my pain, I turned the words of the song towards God and sang them to him. He knew exactly how I felt. I didn't need to try and put it into words. God knew my heart was crying; he knew the turmoil within. When there were few who seemed to understand, he did; and he still does. To have to cope alone would be, for me, a prospect that was virtually impossible; but having God's presence alongside me enables me to keep going each day. I remember hearing a man say, 'We have God and the whole of heaven on our side.' If you cannot gain strength from that, I do not know where else you can. Whether your pain is due to bereavement, an illness, a shattered dream or some other life trauma — the truth of those words from Matthew that were quoted at the beginning of this chapter still ring true. Don't worry about tomorrow, just concentrate on today. After all, you may not have tomorrow. If you do, the God who helps you cope today can give you all the strength necessary for your tomorrow.

3.
Saying goodbye

In the New Testament, death is glorified by the early Christians who longed for Christ's return and came to see their own deaths as a gateway to heaven. But while it might be possible to accept or even welcome the inevitability of our own deaths, it is much harder to come to terms with it when someone we love dies; for those left behind, death is simply horrid. It is unnatural, engulfing, emotionally wrenching, depressing and bleak. Even when we think about where Natalie has gone to, how happy, contented, complete and perfect she is now, that does not alter the ugliness of death itself.

I think it must have been because of the awful nature of our little girl's passing that I quickly began to crave anything beautiful, a contrast to the ugliness of death. Drained by the bleak, dark days that surrounded us, I tried, whenever I was able, to find something beautiful each day.

There is so much beauty in nature. Although I had never really liked the music to the hymn 'Loved with everlasting love', the words kept coming back to me: 'Heaven above is softer blue, earth around is sweeter green'. The hymn is about how nothing looks the same again after you've become a Christian, and you see the world in a completely different light. Once you realize how God provides for us through his creation, everything becomes more beautiful. This hymn took on new significance for me as I suddenly became more aware of the beauty in nature. I noticed flowers — their spectrum of hues seemed to shout at me as I walked or drove by. I even remember remarking to someone at the hospital where Nattie had died, that her death had occurred in possibly the nicest season because everywhere there were flowers. It may have seemed a bit strange to others, but to us it was very meaningful, and so while we were waiting for someone in Alder Hey Hospital, the children and I spent a very special half hour counting all the different colours of clover in the grass.

For Nattie's funeral, or Thanksgiving Service as we preferred to call it, we wanted the flowers to try and bring colour and splendour. All of the children made their own floral tribute for Nattie. I didn't want the extravagant but empty gesture of an impersonal floral display, so we designed our own. I will never forget trying to pick flowers for the service, fighting back the tears as I stood in the large supermarket, desperately trying to make the right decision (as if there was one!), so that the flowers would be perfect.

Our family spent the night before the funeral surrounded by blooms, baskets and oasis, trying to create something special with the help of our friends and extended family. As a creative person, I was determined to make the day as meaningful and beautiful as possible.

Natalie's coffin was white satin, stark and plain, though not offensively so. One of my friends had bought lots of coloured ribbon and I distinctly remember tying bright pink ribbons onto the handles of that coffin late that night, as I prepared myself for the day ahead. I had placed three pink roses (pink was her favourite colour) tied with a simple bow on top of the coffin. I wanted to somehow make the ugliest thing a mother should never have to see possess some vestige of beauty. I wanted to force the day to be intimate and personal in defiance of the indiscriminate nature of death. A friend at the hospital had told me that your child's funeral was really important and you should think about it as if you were planning their eighteenth and twenty-first birthdays, and their wedding all in one. So on that advice, we realized it was important to plan that the day would be filled with beauty.

The order of service we had prepared contained a personal message from Steve and me, as we wanted it to be a keepsake too. I really wanted the front to be pretty so I had two little footprints attached to some textured card. Some really kind young people from our church undertook the enormous task of actually preparing all the orders of service, an example of one of the many practical but significant details taken care of by our wider church 'family', for which we were so grateful.

There were many other little things that contributed to making the service as simple and as beautiful as we could. It seemed only natural. Her life had been wonderful and her death was also beautiful in the sense that she had passed into a far more lovely and brilliant future. We knew God viewed her death as precious so we wanted to mark it in a special way too. It's no small wonder that the Bible says, 'Precious in the sight of the LORD is the death of His saints' (Psalm 116:15). Every person who loves Jesus is a saint, so this was a verse that spoke directly about our own daughter. But in order for us to be able to go to heaven, God had to endure the death of his own Son.

Music was also an important part of Nattie's Thanksgiving Service. We wanted the last piece of music played during the service to be poignant and we chose an old song sung by a new artist. Fernando Ortega has a particularly beautiful version of 'Give me Jesus' and Steve and I agreed it would be the perfect end to the service. Little did we realize that its simplicity and challenging words would speak so powerfully to so many. Space doesn't allow me to relate the stories here, but God again used something simple and beautiful to challenge and inspire others.

Music has such power to evoke emotion and, because for so much of the time I had to put my feelings aside for the sake of my children whose needs had to be put first, listening to stirring lyrics became an important release for me. I found that the lyrics of many songs, both old and new, can be inspirational, motivational and, at times, very comforting. Sometimes I sang along to them, often crying as much as singing, but as I let the tears flow, I felt an internal healing begin to take effect.

Anyone who knows me will vouch for the fact that I love to be creative and that I would usually have something 'on the go' when they came to see me. I wouldn't claim my creations are recognizably things of beauty to everyone, but to me, doing something that was intrinsically creative was important as it enriched my life. The reason why it was important became apparent to me especially at this time. God was able to use his creation, and all the other beautiful and precious things this world can offer, to be of great comfort to me.

That is how I tick; that is how I am made. Others may have different ways of expressing their nature and relating to God that work better for them. To some, spotting a group of delicate wild flowers poking their noses out of the tarmac may even seem a trivial or silly thing, but I have learnt that when everything else around you seems black, it is essential to acknowledge and embrace any wonderful thing, however small it may be, that gives colour to this life, even if you have to force yourself to. No day, however busy, hard or mundane, should pass by without making time to find some moment to pause and thank God for his world and the gifts he gives us all. By looking beyond the sin and tragedy in our lives and giving thanks for his abundant beauty, our weariest days are blessed and made bearable.

4.
Be kind to yourself

Shortly after Natalie died, we received hundreds of wonderfully kind cards. It was so encouraging to read the verses and kind thoughts that people had written to us. One lovely lady sent a card that simply said, 'Be kind to yourself...', and on the inside followed the words, 'you just need time to grieve.'

The day after Nattie had gone to heaven, I took one of my daughters to school. I pushed myself to do this as I knew that going to school would really help her and I also wanted to talk to some of the staff. It was definitely the right thing to do at that moment, but as time went by I started to realize that I needed to reassess all the day-to-day things that I did. I had to consider how far it was necessary to push myself. As a person I've always been pretty 'driven' and so there began a tussle within as I struggled between letting others help me and asking myself how long I should continue to accept their support.

We were receiving an incredible amount of domestic help and I knew it had to be phased out. We had to return to some semblance of normality but the timing was entirely up to us. We joked about how long the help would last but, inside, both of us felt a little uncomfortable, even though we knew that the help was so freely and willingly given. But being kind to myself was not just being able to accept support, it was about getting us back to normal too. Our only chance of surviving Nat's death was if we continued functioning as a family. I had to start picking up the reins again but I was unsure whether I would cope. Being kind to myself ironically meant I had to push myself a little to see if I could manage.

This was fine initially; coping was hard but it gave me a focus. However, as the weeks wore on and the usual family whirlwind routine ensued, I found it very difficult to just keep going. This lesson of being kind to myself was going to be pretty hard to swallow. In order to change the way I did things, *I* would have to change. It ate at my pride and at my need to be self-sufficient. It wasn't just that I needed to be 'self-kind', I had to acknowledge that I needed to put on the brakes and let my diminished timetable of 'things to do' give me the space and time to grieve.

It is a lesson I am still struggling with. Was I capable of giving up some of the things I felt I had to do, in order to spend a little time caring for myself? I found such an idea very difficult to accept, partly because all the things that I did seemed so essential to keeping the family going, and partly because it just went against my principles: it didn't seem right putting myself first, even for just a little while. Wasn't that just the selfish 'me, me, me' approach?

Although I would never have described myself to others solely in terms of being a parent, in common with many women, my sense of identity had shifted once I became a mother. Having children changes you. Inevitably, there were personal sacrifices that had to be made in order to keep up with my five young children. I'm not talking about being some sort of parental martyr. It's just a fact — one that every parent of young children will understand — that once you have children, many juggling acts are necessary in order to see to all their needs; and this juggling intensifies the more children you have. Quite simply, I was used to coming last. I didn't always like it: sometimes I envied the freedom of childless women to be so spontaneous about their social life or visits to the gym. But I accepted it. After all, I didn't want that sort of life any more, I loved being a mother. Yet that didn't stop me sometimes yearning for a little bit of space and time just to recharge my batteries.

Now those batteries weren't just flashing on low, they were practically empty; and here I was with people depending on me to function, at least on some basic level. Much as I felt like it, retreating to the bedroom, pulling the duvet over my head and giving up just wasn't an option: it wouldn't be fair to my husband or the children. Yet neither could I ignore the wrestling within.

Gradually, I realized that to all intents and purposes I was 'sick'. My body, heart and soul had received an enormous jolt and the ramifications of Natalie's death were only just beginning to materialize. I was in need of healing. If I was going to be any sort of decent mother and wife I had to be able to cope myself, and that meant I could no longer ignore my own needs.

In order to grieve, I had to listen to my physiological, emotional and spiritual needs and attend to them. I could not be 'fixed' — I would be altered for ever — but the person I was to become depended on my response to the situation and my ability to take steps to acknowledge the grief process and let it begin. And that would take time.

If you've read any books on grief (and believe you me, I've now read a few) you will quickly realize that you are in territory that is widely researched yet so individual that you cannot predict your own path. One of the best books I read simply listed physiological and emotional responses to grief. I had several 'light bulb' moments that made me suddenly aware and able to understand that the things I had been feeling and doing were entirely normal; and it was such a relief!

For example, the evening of Nat's death I had experienced actual pain in my heart. I had had palpitations and it really felt as if someone was kneeling on my ribcage. That was okay. It was an entirely normal experience. My need to do positive things afterwards, to make sense of her death was also recognized. My husband's reactions, while dramatically different from mine, were completely normal too.

The more I read, the more I had a glimpse into this mysterious condition called grief. I realized that there was no 'quick fix' and that if I was ever to stand a chance of taking care of others, I had to take care of myself. I would love to be able to say that I suddenly ate an incredibly healthy and balanced diet, or that I immediately rearranged my life to include plenty of opportunities to take time out and 'be still', but unfortunately, I can't! There just wasn't the time.

Even so, I began to realize that there were some things that I did not need to do, that it was perfectly alright to say 'no' sometimes and acknowledge instead the things I had to do for myself.

At first, when it just felt too much to go somewhere I was expected, I felt guilty about not turning up. What kind of example would that set for my children? Then I learnt to accept that if going to certain places was just going to upset me more than I could bear, the wisest and kindest thing to do was to stay at home just for then. Burn-out is no feat to be proud of and I think we do well if we acknowledge the warning signs our bodies give us. And that's an important example to set for our children too. When I was fatigued, I had to learn that the best thing to do was to go to bed. When I needed to cry, it was wisest to do just that, even if it meant making other plans to give me the privacy, or embarrassing the people around me by letting myself cry right then and there.

Was it acceptable not to go to certain things? I had to think this through and assess yet again. I'm not suggesting that it's okay generally to live your life without commitment, particularly when it comes to spiritual things, but there are times when your priorities have to change (even if only temporarily). I've been too busy just surviving, sometimes barely keeping my head above water, but I have had to acknowledge that there are some things I need to do for myself. If there have been things I didn't really need to do, I've often chosen not to do them.

Sometimes solitude is crucial but I've not fared so well with this. You just need time out, space and reflection. You need time to read the Bible, and other good books, time to pray and consider how you are doing. I needed 'me' time, not in the selfish sense, but in order to heal. Most of us have to convalesce at some time, and I was no exception. It was not a physical recovery (although that was part of it); I had to make an emotional and spiritual healing that could not be fixed rapidly or haphazardly.

Sometimes 'being kind to yourself' means making time to be with the family, just taking time to talk and be together. But although it was important to grieve together as a family, I was mindful of trying to maintain the delicate balance of our children's grief needs and ours as adults. For example, there were times when I really needed to go and visit Natalie's grave, but some of the children wouldn't want to go. I had to weigh up whose needs were paramount at each opportunity and what the other options were. Mostly, I decided not to go when we were together as some of them found it too distressing, but on some occasions I explained to them that it was something that I really had to do. It is a difficult balance, one that I will not know I have got right until my children are older and they can reflect upon what happened themselves. Trying to achieve that balance has utterly convinced me that we each develop what I call 'grief needs', a certain way in which we need to grieve in order for our bodies, minds and hearts to begin to heal. These are deep wounds, which granulate so slowly and reopen so rapidly. There are no miracle stitches here!

If my own 'grief needs' weren't met, I began to feel frustrated, angry or resentful. The main problem was not feeling free to talk to people about Natalie or how I was feeling. People I spoke to often seemed uncomfortable about the subject, or just avoided it altogether. To some extent, I understood how they felt — death and grief are often taboo subjects of conversation — but it was as if Natalie had begun to be forgotten. When people didn't even mention her, I felt a pain like no other, and the frustration was often more than I could bear. Although I knew deep down that this silence could be put down to people feeling uncomfortable, or wanting to 'spare' my feelings (as if that were possible!), or simply traditional 'British reserve', I began to feel bitter. I *needed* to talk about what had happened but it sometimes felt like others didn't want to listen. Gradually, I realized this was in some ways selfish. Being kind to myself was more than just a nod in the direction of giving myself time out, it was also coming to terms with the fact that it was hard keeping a lid on my frustrations because my innately 'sinful' or 'selfish' nature was being compounded by my grief. Yet again I was looking in the wrong place: to myself and to others instead of to God. I should not have expected other people to fulfil my needs. So I confessed my sin — my resentment and frustration toward others — and asked for God's forgiveness. But, of course, the Lord already knew. He understood everything and, unlike other people, he was always there to listen to me. I began to learn to talk to him and also to search out the people who I knew would really talk to me — and let me ramble too!

A kind friend I'd confided in about this told me it was completely natural and acceptable to be feeling like this. But although it was normal, I still knew the feelings were unhelpful, and that I had to keep asking God to help me to be gracious. Punishing myself for feeling like this was not being kind to myself! I had to be gentle with myself instead and accept that these feelings of resentment and frustration were just the tip of the far deeper and more powerful emotions wrestling inside me.

This lesson of having to treat myself carefully will be one that I will always struggle to learn. It's something many people find hard to do, whether or not they've been bereaved; but when you are grieving, it is especially worth keeping on struggling to maintain that balance of meeting your own needs, as well as those of others. For me, being kind to myself ultimately meant using all available resources to make my life easier, combined with drawing on God's strength and help to get through each day. It's only through depending on him and reading the Bible that my days become more manageable. When I rely on my own strength it is little wonder that the days are such a struggle. I have to keep reminding myself of the verse: 'I can do all things through Christ who strengthens me' (Philippians 4:13). With his strength, the support of others, and being kind to myself, I can make it, one day at a time.

5.
Do something positive

Positive is not really a word that I would use to describe my life right now. I should be; I have an amazing family, wonderful friends, a full and rewarding life and ultimately an eternal future that fills me with hope and comfort. But, positive is something I struggle to be. I have hope. I have assurance. I've had comfort beyond anything I could have envisaged, but it's still so tough to be positive. Positivism takes work and requires a real effort. This is because inside I am still hurting. My emotions are often all over the place and many a time I feel that I have little to look forward to. I'm sorry, I have to be transparent; being brave yet dishonest never really encourages anyone. It's in such moments that something is driving me to seek out positive activities to do. It is another case of my head ruling my heart. My heart would often drive me to despair. My emotions would render me a complete wreck, yet there is a God-given drive that sends me in a different direction. I'm not sounding a call to suppress your grief — no, grief has to be acknowledged; and yes, I know that you have to cry, weep and even rage. Yet it is more than just dismissing how you feel. It isn't simply trying to be brave, because I'm not brave; I'm just extremely good at crying in private. I learned fairly quickly that open, public expressions of grief don't go down that well! There are some wonderful people who accept your tears, but many are obviously uncomfortable. I've often mused that it's probably a British and cultural phenomenon. I have wondered if it would be easier to live in an Eastern country where I could wear black and openly wail! Despite having to learn to drive whilst crying, which is not terribly safe, I've tended to keep my feelings under control in order to feel an accepted part of society. Fortunately, all of these feelings (according to some of the literature on grief that I have read) are entirely normal (phew!), and so also is a desire to do something positive.

If I can try and divert my energies towards making a difference in either my own life or the lives of others, that makes me feel a little better. Because I have no real reason to make sense of Natalie's death, it feels good trying to make her life and death count. I'm outlining a couple of examples that I've been involved with but please do not misconstrue my motives. This is not a self-congratulating process, as when I look at what other people have achieved and campaigned for, I feel thoroughly ashamed at my feeble efforts.

The girls (Suzie and Heather) wanted to raise some money for a meningitis charity and so they decided to hold a cake sale. Their school was kind enough to support their endeavour, so two days and 600+ cakes later we'd raised money in Nat's memory to support that charity. Apart from not wishing to ever bake a cake again, the great feeling that the process engendered was extremely positive and it was a really good project for the girls to do. They felt that they'd done something useful in honour of Natalie and their obvious pride was wonderful to witness.

We've also tried to get involved with helping some of the people and organizations that have been of invaluable help to us. To be able to 'pitch in' in a small way has been extremely rewarding and has enabled us to help repay their kindnesses towards us. As I consider some of the environments we've been in, it makes me think about little improvements that could make big differences. I would love to campaign for changes in the funeral business. I'd love for children to be seen by their families in little beds rather than funeral parlour coffins. I'd welcome less 'funereal' surroundings and more of the kind of environment that some of the wonderful children's hospices provide. The list goes on. I'd love to promote some of the unsung heroes and departments but I need wisdom to know where to invest my time. It's always so true and incredibly ironic, that when you give a little of yourself to others, the investment often pays dividends beyond what you could have imagined.

Sometimes being positive has required me to open myself up to people I wouldn't ordinarily have done. One such occasion involved chatting to a complete stranger in a park. I shared something of what had just happened to us. Unbeknown to me, she was a Christian and since then we have become really good friends.

God has used her to be such an encouragement to me and I would never have got to know her without trying to be positive and pushing myself to go out and talk to new people. She is one good example of Romans 8:28: 'And we know that all things work together for good to those who love God...' God has worked something out of our tragedy for my good. I've gained a friend who has restored my faith in having friendships at more than just a superficial level. There are blessings around the corner that we do not know of. God gives and gives again; sometimes we just have to be looking for the blessings. If I hadn't visited the park that day, my life would be less rich now. It's true that you do need times to withdraw and really grieve, but as soon as you get the slightest vestige of strength, go out; it's worth the risk and the gargantuan effort.

Other attempts at being positive have included *trying* to look beyond my own problems in a small way. I knew that dwelling solely on my own difficulties would only lead to depression. I tried to start asking other people about their own lives. In a note that we sent to our church the weekend after Nat died, we asked people to continue sharing their lives with us.

We still wanted to hear about their problems too as we realized that some might shy away from telling us about their own hardships. We still desperately wanted to feel part of normal church life, as nothing else in our world was normal in any way, shape or form. I distinctly recall going to visit one friend who had just had a baby. I cried all the way there, composed myself, spent time with them and then wept all the way back. It was unbelievably hard and it wasn't that long after Nattie had died. I really examined my motives and knew that I didn't begrudge her any happiness, it was just that this new life forcibly reminded me of the fact that we had lost our little child. It was bittersweet but I knew I had to get past my own feelings, celebrate with others and be positive with them.

Doing positive things has helped me gain more of a hopeful outlook. When I am feeling down, forcing myself into actually doing something has been of great help to me. Fighting negativity remains a constant battle and with God's help I try to hold on to all the great things in my life with gratitude. I will endeavour to live my life in such a way as to make my life count. I will fail, I won't always be positive nor do what I know to be right, but at least I know what I should do. Doing something positive is a tonic for the really tough times. It takes your eyes off yourself for a moment and helps to regain a little of that lost perspective. It's not just an option, it's a necessity.

6.
Be practical and create memories

I often joke that I should have been an American. There is something about the way they celebrate family life and I love their emphasis on memories and traditions. Creating family traditions is something that we enjoy doing. One of our more popular ones is the cookies and milk ritual. Since Suzie began her first day at school I have baked cookies or muffins for the children to have with a glass of milk on the first day of every new term. It helps to ease them into the whirlwind of a new term and I'm rarely allowed to forget about it!

It's only when things are gone that we wish we had a better way of remembering them. We're now in the process of creating our own memories and traditions for keeping our own thoughts about Natalie alive. I had created memory boxes for a couple of people as a wedding gift and it seemed natural to compile one about Nattie. Trying to sort out a minimal amount of poignant items to put into one box is hard, but it has been an important release. I'm still not ready to sort out her clothes; they are all tucked away for a day when I feel much stronger. This box is filled with little fragments of her: locks of hair, a dummy holder, her footprints and handprints, old cards, identity tags and pictures etc. When I need to, I can use the box to remember. My children also have their own memory box full of their own treasured mementoes. Theirs is private and special; just like mine. My husband can rarely bear to look in the memory box which is such a comfort for me, but so painful for him — yet another reminder of the unique and individual walk of grief.

Other treasured possessions were created by other people. As soon as we began planning Nattie's funeral, I asked a friend if she could sort out two books for us. One was a memory book for anyone to write their own rememberings about Natalie. I knew that mine would fade and as much of her life was filled with ordinary and everyday things it was difficult to pluck out many specific memories. At two and a half your supreme achievements and successes are easy to count. They are no less special but there are no medals, certificates or amazing memories of birthdays or other special events. She had only ever had three Christmases and her first was a complete blur to us. She had celebrated two birthdays and we had the photographs, but there aren't many of them. The book that was created is very special to us. It is full of encouraging words and 'snapshots' of Natalie. Many of other people's memories involved conversations or events that we weren't always party to. As we read their thoughts, it helps us to remember that she was special to other people too. Some of these entries provide a release for our emotions.

The other book was completed at Natalie's Thanksgiving Service. It is simply a collection of names of everyone who came to stand with us in our grief that day. I remember so little about the day and I certainly didn't get to meet everyone who attended.

Be practical and create memories

This book is a record of all the wonderful and kind people who shared in our sorrow and came to say goodbye to Natalie. It is very precious. When I am tempted to think that people have forgotten and do not care, this book refutes these feelings. It tells me that I am cared about indeed.

As time has gone on and life seems to become a little more normal, it's easy to try and suppress our grief. You cannot function by keeping emotional wounds constantly open; there has to be a level of coping. I think that perhaps you can measure some of your progress in the healing process by how painful everyday life feels. However, as the length of time since Nat died has increased, there has also been the temptation not to think about her too much because you become weary of the grief. This isn't a form of denial, just a coping mechanism. But my heart told me that I needed to create a release too. When I'm feeling sad I turn to my memory box or book and the tears soon begin to flow. The memories flood back and the pain re-emerges. Whilst I could not do this every day, I sense that keeping emotion locked away will only be harmful for me.

Despite few people now asking me how I am and Natalie being mentioned by only a handful of really good friends, I must not and cannot forget her. That is why my memories are so valuable; they link me with my past and remind me that the future is something to look forward to. I am grateful to God for my memory. Funnily enough, it is not something that I've ever previously had cause to thank him for. He created my body so perfectly knowing that memory not only gives a sense of place and person, but gives unbelievable comfort to all of us who have been bereaved.

There are many other memories that I want to create — traditions involving remembering Nat, and new things that give us a sense of family. I have spent many hours in the process of compiling a scrapbook. Scrapbooking is becoming very popular in the UK and is little more than an illustrated photo album with space to record times, dates, details and thoughts. I have one partially completed about Natalie and have spent much time creating a lovely pictorial capsule about her. It has been extraordinarily painful sorting through photographs, trying to recall how we felt at the time and where we were when the pictures were taken.

Not only has it been a healing process for me and an extension of my personal grief, but it also stands as a record that is there for all to see. My children love to flick through the pages and it helps trigger memories for them. They talk of her, they laugh, they feel sad and her memory is kept alive in them. As Jamie (Natalie's twin brother) was so little when she died, this book is for him too. I hope that it will help him as he grows and he struggles to remember her. I have loved creating something that I can cherish; that is as beautiful as I can make it — something to remember her by.

There are other projects waiting for my spare time. I have a memory blanket waiting to be assembled. It will be a patchwork of material with photos of her and us fused into the fabric. When I need to, I'll be able to snuggle in this quilt and feel comforted.

There will be some of you reading this that have absolutely no desire to be creative. Perhaps you would prefer to initiate family traditions that will mark important dates instead.

We wanted to accent Natalie's funeral with markers that included the children. We knew that the day would be painful and confusing, and so wanted to convey to them that we had to say goodbye to her. In light of the fact that my children were very young, we realized that it needed to be symbolic and hopefully would also give them a sense of being part of the day rather than just onlookers. We wanted to include them during the service and had a friend sing the song 'Jesus loves me this I know' that Nattie and Jamie had sung every night before they slept. Their main inclusion was to be at the graveside. I remember all too well the long walk to the grave. The way that God had answered our prayer for a perfect plot is another story, but we had a really beautiful place provided by a kind church not far from the girls' school.

Once the committal was over, we gave each child one pink helium-filled balloon, and I explained again to the children that although we had just lowered Natalie's body into the ground, the real Natalie was up in heaven. As they let go of the balloons, I asked the children to try and say goodbye to her. We said that just as the balloons would go upwards, so we needed to remember that Nattie was up in heaven. We cut the weights and each of the children let their balloons go. We told them that just as we were letting the balloons go, we also had to let Natalie go. She wasn't here any longer. It was only her shell that we had lowered into the ground. The real Natalie was alive and she was alive in heaven. Everyone watched them rise and disappear out of view. It was personal, poignant and intensely special.

When it came to Jamie's birthday (which would have obviously been hers too), I wanted to repeat the exercise. Each of us went to a florist and chose some special birthday balloons. This time, I gave each one a parcel tag and asked them to write (or tell me) what they would have liked to say to her on her birthday. I had to carefully explain that Natalie couldn't read them nor would know what we had expressed but we were doing it to help us and to give us a way to describe how we were feeling. We all went down to the grave, early, before school, and one by one we read what we had written. It was such an emotional moment and even Jamie tried to cry. As we watched the balloons ascend we all sang 'Jesus loves me this I know' while we held each other's hands. That day was long, but it felt as if we had done something positive. You do not remember individual tears and rarely specific emotions but when I remember that day, I recall being sad but being together as a family. Those recollections are priceless and well worth repeating.

Traditions can bring personal meaning to a specific event. As time hurtles on and my memory recalls less of the awful events surrounding her death, I want to orchestrate times that honour her memory. These times need also to be a reminder of the fact that we are still incredibly fortunate and blessed beyond our realization. Our thanks for our lives and for each other need to be turned toward God. Hopefully our family remembrances and traditions will in turn honour him too.

7.
Beginning again

Do you ever wish you could change your life? Do you long for things to be different — easier or simpler? My frequent attempts to try and simplify my often chaotic life were rarely successful. Somehow, I was neither strong nor assertive enough. I felt I was simply being carried along by my schedule. It was the 'fighting fires' kind of life. Whilst I did make plans and organize, I never really felt that events were under any sort of control. Whilst I know that God is ultimately in control, that my times are in his hands (Psalm 31:15) and he will direct my path (Proverbs 3:6), God has also given me free will. I do not really honour him if I lurch from one thing to another without really considering if it is the best way of living my life. There are so many good activities that my family and I can get involved with, but are they a good use of my time and am I becoming too busy to focus on my priorities? I think that attaining the right balance is one of the hardest things I have to do in my life and I really wish that you knew when you had achieved it!

If anything is worth having, then it must be worth striving for. Asking the question of how God would have me live this life is worthwhile. It can help dictate what I regard as important. I'm not talking about principles that I live my life by, but the way I choose what I should do. It suddenly became obvious one day that through Nat's death, God had really given me the opportunity to reassess my priorities. Ironically you become a little untouchable when you are bereaved. People expect you to behave a little differently whether they agree or understand it, or not. So, could I use the fact that things had changed, and my schedule was temporarily altered, to make some permanent adjustments? I had bought a book called *The Too-Busy Book* (by Linda Anderson) and it had really made me think about what was 'necessary' and what was 'less important'.

I am by nature a 'people pleaser' and I find it very hard to say no to things. There were many things in my life that were good but not necessarily vital. I now had a chance to sift all activities through a finer sieve and see which ones were valuable. Deciding between 'good' and 'best' is hard, but I knew that I had to be mature, stand up for myself and my family, and act as a gatekeeper. It was vital to keep certain things away from our schedules in order to let us 'breathe'. There were some excellent activities that we were involved with and there was pressure to slot in even more. My children regularly asked to attend more and more activities and I needed to say no to some of them for the good of us all. Otherwise, when would we get opportunities to be together, rest or recover? I'm not advocating a leisure-filled life, nor a retreat from responsibility, but I was not convinced by the supposed benefits of some seemingly good things. I started asking myself some questions. How was it going to impact me? Would flitting from one activity to the next increase the stress on all of us? And what would the children really gain from it? Did my children, husband or I have space to just be ourselves and not be crowded out with overstimulation? It is tempting to judge my parenting success by the fulness of my children's schedules, but do they really need to be that busy and is it good for them?

I started to ask myself some introspective questions. How much time for myself did I need? Would I be a better mother by taking time out to think, pray, read and assess my situation? When I looked at Christ's example, there were times when he got away from everything to spend time with God. When I'm too busy to do the same, whose fault is that? God gave us one day of rest each week, so why didn't I take advantage of it?

I realized that saying no would prove to be liberating but also very scary. How would I refuse, and how would I explain my actions? As I'm not accountable to absolutely everyone, I knew that I needed to be more mature. I had to resist the temptation to justify my decisions so that people wouldn't think badly of me. There's the 'people pleasing' problem again. I'm often more bothered about what others will think of me than asking myself what God might think about my choices. Letting people potentially misunderstand me is hard for me — but I only have one life and on the day when I have to account for the way I have lived it, the responsibility will fall entirely on my shoulders. That's what I've learned in a very stark manner. I have one solitary life and it will be over before I know it. Nat's life was incredibly short and I do not have tomorrow as a guarantee. Some of these 'things to do' are often pushed over until the next day in a procrastinatory manner. But what if I don't have tomorrow? What if my future next week involves meeting God face-to-face? Am I really ready to leave this life and know that I've done what I need to do?

Once you begin to think like this, priorities start to become clearer. People are important, housework really isn't. Whilst for the sake of my family (and their health) I cannot live in squalor, but is having a 'show home' the best use of my time? Whilst some shopping is vital and enjoyable, is window shopping for present comforts making a difference for eternity? Where am I storing up treasure and am I doing everything in my power to be a light for Christ amongst my family and friends? Do I have friends that I'm spending time with and am I encouraging them?

These priorities started to become crystal clear. The problem then was sifting through my decisions and seeing how they related to my priorities. This was never going to be easy. God had really given me a gift, a chance to change and be true to what I knew was important. I had a golden opportunity to begin again and I had to take it and thank God for it. I wish that I could be more consistent and a little more strategic but I've made small steps of improvement. It's an evolving process and one that I need to ask God for his wisdom in dealing with. I long for God's approval and have to ask him to help me live my life in a way that is best for my family and really pleasing to him.

8.
Learning to grieve differently

One of the hard parts about losing someone you love is not knowing how you are going to react to the news. I had seen television programmes where people had been given bad news about a person having died and had wondered how I would react in the same situation. You cannot really second-guess yourself and you certainly cannot do it for others. I quickly learned that my response and Steve's at any given time was likely to differ. Part of this difference is a matter of being female and male, and some of it can be attributed to our individual personalities. We both coped the only way we knew how. Our differences were to be carefully respected and the realization that we each had vastly differing needs was patently evident. Looking back, it is amazing to see how rarely we were both in such complete despair that we could not offer support or solace to each other.

Steve was an incredible support for me and took some of the really tough jobs upon himself. He was the one who dealt with the coroner. He gave a compulsory statement to the police as he knew I couldn't have managed it. Steve went to pick up the death certificate and did the more dreadful jobs surrounding bereavement. I am so grateful for his strength and care. He saw that I needed people around me: people who could let me talk and cry, or simply distract me. But he really didn't want all that attention and preferred sometimes to be by himself. So I had to learn to look out for his needs too.

I recall one day, a few days before Natalie's funeral, when we had met with many people. Visitors kept coming to our home (about twenty-five that day alone!), and whilst we were both immensely grateful for their care, I could see that Steve had had enough company for the day. So we posted a message on the door, explaining that we would love to see visitors the next day, but we were so very tired now. It was crucial to care for each other and somehow God gave each of us immeasurable amounts of grace to cope. This does not mean, however, that we weren't under strain and that we didn't have to work really hard at sorting out misunderstandings; and we often had to ask forgiveness from each other and from God.

Any literature about coping after someone has died will emphasize the fact that you will grieve uniquely. You have to give each other time and space to adjust to your new reality and expecting your husband to completely understand you or always be strong for you is a tall order. Communication was so important; even if we didn't understand each other, at least if I knew how Steve was feeling, I was better equipped to handle his emotions and not pile my expectations on him too readily. Because the first week or two was such a blur, it was hard to remember what I had said or did on any given day, and making sure we talked to each other meant we could try to avoid misunderstandings.

Sometimes, though, I had to remember that ultimately God was the one who was going to be my complete rock: 'The LORD is my rock and my fortress and my deliverer; my God, my strength, in whom I will trust; my shield and the horn of my salvation, my stronghold' (Psalm 18:2). I leaned heavily on Steve but the only one who completely understood and had infinite supplies of grace and strength was my Father God. He ultimately is the glue in our marriage and he has graciously helped us to come through this tragedy together.

9.
Be grateful

'Why?' That word, which came again and again in many different forms, was a question I found very difficult to respond to. For some, it was an incredulous 'Why?' Why should this happen to people who said they were Christians? Or as one person put it, 'How can this happen to people who claim to be close to God? If you are closer to him than the rest of us, how could he possibly let you suffer in this way?' Some, looking at people around them who appeared not to care very much about their families, wondered why this should happen to a family who so clearly enjoyed being together. Others simply said it wasn't fair that Natalie should have died while wicked people who do so much evil in the world carry on living. Mostly, people were just puzzled, even long-standing Christians. It didn't seem to make any sense. Why would God take a little child to be with himself? Why was her life cut short? Was there really a purpose behind it and, if so, how could we make sense of it all?

Of course, we had many of these thoughts too, but I think the fact that, for the past twelve years, I have had to learn to live with a chronic illness caused me to have a slightly different approach to the question. Although it can be controlled with medication, my condition comes and goes with no rhyme nor reason, and as a result I have just had to learn to accept it, sometimes grudgingly, rarely graciously. I have not really ever seen the need to ask why I had this illness, which is more than a little inconvenient and often stops me functioning at the level that I desire; it has been enough for me just to deal with it and get on with life. With my condition, I've learnt there's never going to be any answers, however long and loud I could shout that question 'Why?', so I've coped best by not asking. As a consequence of dealing with my illness in this way, I suppose that it seemed logical to deal with Nat's death in this manner too.

Don't misunderstand me — I've not willingly and contentedly accepted her death, nor have I refused to grapple with the question of God's sovereignty, of why, if God is all powerful and all loving, he allows such things to happen. Do I wish it could have happened differently? Yes, yes, and another resounding yes! But if I ask 'Why?' what answer do I get? God and heaven are deafeningly silent. I can try to stand back and guess at the bigger picture, but it will only ever be that: guesswork. This is not to say that it hasn't been really helpful to wrestle a little in trying to understand the sovereignty of God, or at least *begin* to understand. It has also been invaluable thinking through how I should respond to other people's questions.

I'm not going to attempt a treatise on the question of suffering as there are many better thinkers and authors than me who have already written about it. I've listed some helpful titles on a dedicated web site, www.emptyarmswithhope.co.uk. They all consider the big questions such as: 'Why doesn't God protect Christians more than those who don't love him?' and

'Why doesn't God stop people dying and, if he did, where would he draw the line in control over other events?' It all seems to come down to why God seems to want our free and unconditional love and not our forced allegiance; and that is really worth dwelling on.

Rather than despair about ever finding an answer to why Nattie had died so terribly young, I found it more useful to dwell on the positives instead. I'm not suggesting for one moment that I haven't been negative, nor am I saying that those feelings are wrong. It's completely natural and normal to feel despair and to think that you will never smile again. I have had very bleak times but I have been fortunate that so far they've not run into days and weeks. They come little and often and I'm learning to allow the grief to heal me by letting my hurting heart cry while looking to my Saviour who has promised to comfort me in all my distress.

Despite the hardship, there is also acknowledgement of God's goodness. I have not been happy, I have been desolate; but I have not been completely in despair because the joy of my salvation, the care of my Lord and the comfort provided by the Bible and my friends have all consoled me.

In the early days after Nattie's death, although at the time I was not convinced that I could cope, when I look back, I can now trace how God's guiding and compassionate hand provided for us a way ahead that we could manage. I know that the Bible says that we will not be tempted or tested beyond what we can bear, but if we rely on our own human resources, we would soon crumble. The enormity of the situation meant that we had to throw ourselves on the mercy of him who loves us and rely on him to uphold us. The verse says, 'No testing has overtaken you that is not common to everyone. God is faithful, and he will not let you be tested beyond your strength, but with the testing he will also provide the way out so that you may be able to endure it' (1 Corinthians 10:13, NRSV); and as we went over again and again every small detail of Nattie's death, we came to realize that God had indeed been faithful and not left us to cope alone.

For example, the day before Nat died, we had spent the morning at our church Toddler Group where she was clingy and spent most of the time on my knee. How grateful I am for all those last cuddles. Then later that evening, after I'd returned from going out, I woke her to give her medicine when I could have decided not to disturb her sleep. I'm so grateful I didn't leave her sleeping or I would have always regretted not checking her. My husband also went to her in his normal round of checking all the children, listening, as parents do, to their breathing, to ensure they were sleeping peacefully. Nothing was out of order, so we can have none of the regrets that we might have had if we had not done those things. Also, I can rest in the knowledge that Nattie received medical attention as quickly as it was possible. As we sped towards the hospital I remember being grateful that the hospital was only five minutes' drive away from our home and that there was an ambulance free. I am incredibly grateful that she didn't die at home or in the ambulance so that every effort that could have been made by the hospital to save her life was indeed made. We were also really thankful that her suffering was very short and we were spared the prolonged agony of a bedside vigil.

God was merciful to us in her death and equally loving in its wake. The provision of the care and kindnesses of the hospital's bereavement services was something that I will always thank God for. I cannot begin to measure how much they helped by supporting us and helping us think through the right kind of questions to ask and what preparations to make. They helped us to understand a little of what our children would be going through, and provided a facility where we could go and see Natalie's body. To hold your child after he or she has died, and to be able to spend time with them then, may seem macabre to some; yet this was our provision for the beginning of our healing. We saw again and again how events leading up to her death had unknowingly helped us to prepare for her passing.

For example, a few weeks earlier, I had watched a documentary about a family living in America who were caring for a large number of adopted children who all had varying physical and mental needs. Part of the programme related how one of their children had died. It showed a couple of black and white photographs which had been taken as a record of some of the events immediately after the little boy's death. One stood out in my memory: a picture of the father carrying his precious little boy in a blanket out to the undertaker's car. He had refused to let them take his son out in a body bag and wanted to carry the little boy out himself. At first I'd looked at the picture feeling puzzled as to why he would have had it photographed, and I felt I was intruding on a very private moment. Then I realized that the family would treasure those photos for ever. The programme had made me cry but had also inspired me by the way that they had coped with the challenges of his death and with bringing up so many children with different difficulties. I would never have guessed that in a matter of weeks I would be holding my daughter in the same way.

Just after we had told our other children that Nattie had died, we all had to go back to the hospital. I immediately remembered the documentary and asked my father-in-law if we could borrow his camera. The pictures of us holding our little girl are some of the most precious I own. How grateful I am now that I watched that programme which helped prepare me and gave me the idea to bring a camera. These thoughts could only have been prompted by God and those bittersweet pictures stand as a record of what happened and the final time that we were able to hold her properly.

We were incredibly thankful for the amount of help, cards, food, cleaning and thoughtfulness we received as a family. Our own immediate family and friends were so vital in caring for us at a time when we were scarcely able to look after ourselves. Our church family were also amazing and really took the time to consider the things that we would really need and find helpful. This was done out of love but it is not something that is unique to our church or situation. We didn't receive all of this care because we were 'paid-up' members of an exclusive club, we were just on the receiving end of care from people who were showing us Christ's love in a very practical way. There are so many churches across the world who do exactly the same thing whether people attend the church or not. Our church would have striven to help us whether we were strangers, had just started attending, or had been there for twenty years.

I could relate many other examples of God's providence and how we came to see his care and guidance in the detail of our circumstances, but it was not something that came easily or naturally to us. However, the alternative was sliding into bitterness and I knew that by counting our remaining blessings I could steal myself away from utter despair. Now, when we look back, we find a tapestry interwoven with grief and goodness. We did not have one without the other and yet our sadness enabled us to learn more how God continues to work all things together for our good, even though in this life we may never know why.

10.
Let the Bible inspire you

Sometimes, clinging on is all you can do. God prepares us for events when we scarcely know about it. I had spent the few months before Nattie's death attending a weekly women's Bible study, where we were making an in-depth study of the book of Genesis: how it fitted in with God's redemptive plan, how the origins of all biblical principles are founded there; and it included a study of the real people found in the book. I had learned so much and found that many of the men and women written about gave real inspiration and comfort to me. Joseph was one such character. As his life unfolded and many difficult and seemingly unfair events happened, he survived because he clung to the words that God had given him — promises of a different future and assurances of his help and faithfulness.

Ironically, the night before Natalie died, our group had been sharing about the sorts of things that they feared. Two of the women spoke of how they feared losing their children. I had fears, but I rarely thought about, nor feared, my children's deaths. Yet the next morning that very scenario was to be mine. Little did I realize that I would be sharing what I had learnt the previous evening with a nurse just hours later. As I waited in the Parents' Room, whilst the nursing staff attended to Natalie, somehow God gave me the strength and peace of mind to share the truth that no matter what would happen, God was in control and, just like Joseph, I had to trust God. Looking back it seems incredulous that as she lay dying I was able to testify to God's goodness, yet it was nothing to do with me and *all* about his enabling. As time seemed to slow in those days and weeks to come, the book of Genesis became very precious to me. The lessons I had learned, and people I had studied, suddenly became very real. I remember a few weeks later I had returned to the Bible study but felt unable to join in with the group discussion. As I sat in the foyer I began to read some of the psalms. Through my tears I felt a real empathy with David as he poured out his heart to God. I read psalms where David cried, laying his heart bare before God. I suddenly related to them in a very raw way. Things that I had never really noticed before were 'jumping' out at me as I read them. It wasn't that I gained some new revelation or understood the Bible more; it was that I now identified with some of God's people differently.

I needed to learn from characters in God's Word. Clinging to God's promises was never going to be easy. Joseph suffered incredibly, often through no fault of his own, yet he had to trust God in times of real difficulty. He had to wait during indeterminably long trials with no apparent end in sight and still remain faithful to the one who had always been faithful to him. Suddenly it was me. I too was in a trial that had no end in sight and the question was whether *I* could be faithful. Fortunately, God was the one keeping hold of me and, when my faith was wavering, he was the one who was never going to let me go. His steadfast love was new every morning, whether mine was or not. I was, and still am, incredibly thankful that my salvation and eternal security is never going to rest on my ability to please him. I cannot rely on my goodness; the Bible tells me it is all as filthy rags (Isaiah 64:6). Fortunately my standing before God is secured by Christ's righteousness and I will always thank him for this.

As I thought about other characters in Genesis, I remembered Abraham and Isaac, and Abraham's willingness to obey God in giving his son as a sacrifice. It was never going to have been required (although Abraham didn't know that God was not going to need him to follow it through to the end as God provided a ram instead) but his obedience to God had always amazed me. I could never have willingly done something like that, yet I had had to lose my own child. I marvelled and then I began to think about God's sacrifice. He willingly gave up his only Son for me. His gift cost him so much and it made me thank God and also wonder at the pain it must have brought to him. He had to send his one and only Son into a world that would ridicule, ill-treat and ultimately murder him. Yet God punished his Son and he did it to save me. As we regularly think about God's amazing plan to redeem us when we share communion at church, I can't help but be amazed at God's sacrifice and Christ's willingness to offer himself for a world of people that rarely give him a second thought. Fortunately, I'm not asked to give that kind of sacrifice. All I'm required to do is to be faithful. I will never be a hero of faith; there is no Hebrews 11 on my life today, but maybe all that God is looking for is my response. As one friend commented to me, Satan wants me to curse God. He wants me to blame God for everything that happened and to tell others around that it's God's fault. I do not understand; I do not see how Nat's death makes any sense but I cannot openly blame the one who saved, kept and blessed me. The only thing I can seem to do now is to cling to him.

I have to remind myself constantly of how faithful God has been to me over the years. You do often have to separate your heart from your head. You have to remove what you are feeling from what you know to be true. Emotions continue to run high yet the only way ahead is to focus on God's Word and everything that I *do* understand. Meditating on God's Word really helps during the times when your heart overwhelms you, even if it is a struggle to read the Bible.

As I reread the book of Job, I began to have a sense of deep respect for a man that I had not considered in much depth. My heart felt his sorrow and, as I read, my admiration for his dignity, courage, transparency and yet his determined love for God increased. People have often been very scathing of Job's wife and her comment to Job: 'Do you still hold fast to your integrity? Curse God and die!' (Job 2:9). Yet as I tried to imagine her grief, which was far greater than my own, I could not be as harsh in my criticism. Here was grief talking; she was bereft, desperate, and her cry to Job was probably more natural than many people care to admit. That is what I have grown to love more about the Bible. It does not gloss over people's humanity and struggle; they are there for our learning *and* our comfort. Job's friends were caring, although a little insensitive, and they made incorrect assumptions about Job, God and his situation. Does that not sound like us? I've often said the wrong thing in an attempt to be comforting. Yet through his friends' blunderings I recognize their care for him and maybe my view of them softens too.

Job and his family are great people to learn from, and when all crashes down around you, it is a relief to read of others who have already been through it.

I want to encourage you to take a close look at one of the men or women in the Bible and ask yourself what you can learn from them. It might be David's dependence and honesty before God as so much around him seemed bleak. It might be the depression of Jonah or the desperation of Jeremiah. God put these people and their histories in his Word to help us and I do well if I follow their examples. When I remember characters from the Bible, it encourages me to keep trusting. Time and time again, their struggles during pain and hardship serve to remind me that God remains in control and he is a rock to those that stand firm on him. The morning of Natalie's death, I shared with the lady who teaches each week at the Bible study about my empathy with Jacob. During that awful morning, I suddenly felt that, like Jacob, I too had been left with a limp. As Jacob had wrestled with God that night, he refused to let God go until he blessed him. This is my desire too — I cannot let go of God; and I trust that he will continue to bless me.

11.
Heaven

My family and I were sitting in a car park the other day, talking about Nattie and how she now knows more than we do. We remembered how she used to sing 'Twinkle Twinkle Little Star' and mused that now she probably knows each star by name! She never went to school, she couldn't read or write, yet now her knowledge of everything is vaster than the wisest scholar this world can muster. She used to sing enthusiastically (if a little off pitch!), yet now she can worship in perfect harmony and understands completely. She had no grasp of time; now she dwells in a place where there is none. Her short life here was measured in days, weeks and months; her life in heaven is simply immeasurable in its eternity. In a way, it's wonderful to think she was spared much of the heartbreak and pain of this earthly life; we suffer, but she will never have to endure having such a heart wrench.

Our pastor spoke at her Thanksgiving Service about all the things that she would miss, which had been on my mind a lot. I imagined her first day at school, learning to read, shopping trips with all my four girls, her first boyfriend, her wedding, her babies. But then he looked at it another way. He said when we get to heaven, she will greet us with, 'Look at what *you've* missed!' We will never experience as much of heaven as Natalie will: she has beat us to it! She is the fortunate one. She has been spared experiencing the pain of rejection, self-doubt, cruelty from others, ridicule, nor will she see her dreams collapse around her, or despair at the self-destruction of those she loves.

When Nattie died, heaven suddenly became a very real and special place for me. I have to confess that, before then, although I was glad I knew I would go to heaven one day, beyond that I thought little more about it: I was quite happy with life here and now. I lived as if this world was the centre stage and heaven was just the encore. I was too comfortable in this world and my attitude was so wrong. All of us have to face this some time in life; for me, Nattie's death was a big 'reality check'; one I'd much rather not have had.

However, after Nattie had left us, I couldn't stop thinking about heaven. It was where she was now and I wanted to talk and think about heaven continuously. As I've mentioned before, in the first few days our family and our wider church 'family' looked after us amazingly. They called and cared, cleaned and comforted, and basically saw to all our practical and physical needs; but in terms of our spiritual and emotional needs, there was still something missing.

I will never forget the night before the funeral. It was so long and so hard. The day had been inordinately difficult in many ways and as a family we were completely exhausted. Grief and exhaustion are a horrible combination and I was completely at my wits' end. I couldn't sleep, so I went downstairs to be by myself for a while. One of my best friends had made me promise that if I couldn't sleep, I must ring her. Thank God for wonderful friends! Through my tears I just asked if she would talk to me about heaven. As we talked, we got out our Bibles and she read me Revelation 21; and my heart was incredibly comforted.

The next day at the funeral I spoke to another friend and asked if she would come and visit me and just talk about heaven too. Natalie's death had awakened something inside me. Thoughts of heaven were constantly in my heart and on my mind. How could I not want to find out about and picture the place where my little daughter now lived?

One thing is for certain, I knew what heaven wasn't. I was sure it was nothing like it is conventionally portrayed as a place in the clouds where angelic-looking people with wings sit around strumming harps and looking decidedly bored! Heaven is not boring. Heaven will be amazing, or more accurately, heaven *is* amazing — it's not some 'pie in the sky, by and by, after we die', existing only in the future; it exists now. I am sure of this because when I became a Christian, God accepted me into his family since Christ's death paid the punishment for my sin. Heaven is my definite guaranteed destination, not an allocation on arrival like some holiday deal where you're never too sure where you'll end up!

As I began to picture heaven, my heart was uplifted. To find out more, we read books (there are some really helpful ones which I have listed on the web site, www. emptyarmswithhope.co.uk), and we reread the Bible. You only have to take a brief look into the book of Revelation and its descriptions of our eternal home to be transported to a place of wonder. Read Revelation chapter 21 and be prepared to marvel! I love the fact that this God-breathed scripture allows us just a glimpse of heaven. It is as though the reality of heaven will be just so wonderful it is beyond our grasp to fully comprehend it now other than by the words that feed our spirit with its imagery. Can you imagine a city of pure gold, like clear glass (v. 18)? There's nothing like that here on earth! The foundations of the city walls drip with all kinds of precious stones and there's no need for light because the Lamb (Jesus) is the light — a light that never fades (v. 23). There is no more death, no pain, no grief. There is no sin, no sickness. Think about it: that means there's no need for doctors, or therapists, let alone fitness experts, cosmetic surgeons, self-help gurus or exercise regimes! No alarm clocks, ovens, vacuums, washing machines, and no need for mechanics to mend them when they break down either. Won't heaven be simply wonderful! No one will miss these things, which are so much to do with our feeble, human attempts to cope in a fallen world. But what about eternity? What does the Bible say about that?

In eternity, I will see Nattie face to face. In eternity, bereavement finishes. No wonder I was so looking forward to it! I was reminded of the Old Testament story in which King David has lost a baby son. He speaks of his hope of his son being in heaven: 'But now he is dead; why should I fast? Can I bring him back again? I shall go to him, but he shall not return to me' (2 Samuel 12:23). Just as an alcoholic who has conquered his addiction always describes himself as a recovering alcoholic, so a bereaved parent never refers to their bereavement in the past tense; both know they struggle to survive one day at a time. It is a long, slow journey. The beginning was sudden and jolting, but the middle seems never-ending. Where is the end? When do I finish being bereaved and when does it all get better? In eternity.

In those first few days and weeks, eternity seemed so real it felt tangible, as though I could almost reach out and touch it. The mere thought of Nattie perhaps skipping around heaven singing praise to God in that inimitable way of hers was so comforting. Then I wondered, is that how she will really be now? I know she will be mature in Christ, perfect, but does that mean she is instantly older? I don't know, and, in a way, I'm so glad that I don't. I can think of her as she was but know also that she will not remain as a two and a half year old. When I see her in heaven, she will have reached her full potential and attained her perfect, heavenly body that will make our own, frail human bodies seem like worn-out tents in comparison. She will mature but no one knows how quickly, for with God a thousand years is as one day, and one day as a thousand years (2 Peter 3:8).

God is sovereign over everything, and that includes time. How could our finite, human minds comprehend that? Isn't God so kind not to overburden us with such mind-blowing knowledge? It is enough for me to wonder and to thank God that Nattie is safe in eternity with him.

To see Nattie again was all that I longed for, yet the Lord gently reminded me that heaven is not just about Natalie. He allowed me this glimpse of eternity, then gradually turned my gaze towards him and the joy of seeing my Saviour and my King face-to-face.

You see, if we live with heaven in our hearts, it changes all our plans and our goals. It makes us see this world for all that it is and reminds us that this life is not all there is. If heaven really is my destination, I need to think more about making my life count. Trying to find the words to express something meaningful on Natalie's gravestone was so difficult. More difficult still was trying to sum up her small and tiny but so significant life into a tribute to be read at her funeral. It made me look ahead and wonder what might be put on my own headstone and what people will say about me. Will I have achieved anything significant to write about? I have not done anything that people would think remarkable. But human accolades aren't actually that important. If I have heaven as my daily reality, then all that matters in my life is how it is evaluated by

God. The only affirmation I really need is to hear him say, 'Well done, good and faithful servant' (Matthew 25:21).

So I look forward and onwards, journeying towards heaven. That is our destination; that is our goal. And just as Natalie is blameless, sinless, perfect and mature in Christ, so will I be, since Jesus is my Saviour and there is no fear in love, not even fear of death. What a wonderful thought that three of my children will be there to welcome me into my eternal home — not just Nattie, but the two little babies I lost before they were born. Their shortened lives are now eternal lives and one day I *will* be there with them.

> When God gets us alone by affliction, heartbreak or temptation, by disappointment, sickness, or by thwarted affection, by a broken friendship or a new friendship — when He gets us absolutely alone, and we are dumbfounded and cannot ask one question, then He begins to expound
>
> (Oswald Chambers).

12.
The journey continues

I had been for another appointment at the hospital where Natalie had died. It was for one of my daughters and completely unrelated to Nattie. Sometimes coming back to the hospital was easy, other times it felt extremely tough. Today it was hard, so very hard. The children wanted to play in the hospital playground. There is a section that has been designed as a garden, surrounded by benches and pergolas. I sat in this 'oasis' and began to cry. Sometimes the feeling just overwhelms you; it is like a blanket being slowly lowered over you and you just have to give in to the enveloping emotions. Through my tears I noticed a cabbage white butterfly fluttering through some lavender. I was suddenly struck by the brevity of its life. This butterfly lives for about two weeks and yet its short life is meaningful and purposeful. Its days are full and happy yet no one mourns its passing. God created that tiny life and he cares about it.

I thought about Natalie and how short her life was. God made her — beautiful in her entirety even with the little differences that made her unique. Yet her life was purposeful and meaningful. She taught us through her life and she is still teaching us through her death. She showed us how to love her as a complete individual. She gave us the opportunity to learn patience and, particularly in the early days after her (and Jamie's) birth, she taught us to rely on God's sustaining power as exhaustion threatened to consume us. Yet she taught us much more than this and her sometimes quiet but often shy personality was how God had designed her.

Time is passing quickly. This book had been completed, and yet my life has now begun a new chapter that challenges my emotions once more. God has gifted our family with a new life. As I write, I am seven months pregnant. What seemed initially a wonderful gift to fill us with hope has also awakened many new feelings that I was quite unprepared for.

I have had time to wonder and to give thanks for God's great gift to us; yet it remains at deep contrast to Natalie. Sometimes despite knowing that she is eternally alive, her death feels like an aching full stop rather than a comma. It seems unfair that this baby will never have known her. It brings back memories of her as a baby, and it has made me long for her more.

Others have seen this baby as 'healing' for our family. I suppose it is tempting for them to feel that now we will be okay. I often wish that people could glimpse my heart and see how ragged it remains. How it still aches so deeply and often feels so empty. I have felt so much anguish about welcoming this wonderful new life into our family, feeling somehow that we are glossing over Natalie's memory.

Yet in all of this, God has chosen to give us one more child. I have another reason to continue striving to be the best that I can, and honouring God with my life.

God has shown his kindness so perceptively at times throughout my pregnancy. I hadn't really considered the impact of what sex the baby would be. Amazingly the second and third scans were performed by a lovely woman who turned out to be another parent at the girls' school. I really needed some sensitivity at this time and when the sonographer told me that this baby was to be a boy, it was wonderful news. I mused what this new information about the baby meant. I would not be comparing our new 'life' so much with Nattie now we knew it was a 'him'! It didn't feel like we were replacing her in any way and even some more practical decisions were eased, such as what we would have done with Nattie's clothes. I couldn't have dressed a new addition in her old outfits but I would have found it equally hard purchasing lots of little girls' things. God had provided a little brother for Jamie, somebody new and very different and hopefully one who will grow up to be a great friend and support to him in the future. God has been so gentle and kind without me realizing it. He knew what would have further distressed me and he saved me from it.

I've commented so often that it feels like bereavement has made me a worse person than I was before. It has often magnified my sin and unworthiness. But maybe

I am more use to God as a bruised reed. In a small way, if I can glorify him in my obvious weaknesses then that is preferable to trying to please him in my own strength. I better understand now the verse that talks of the weak things of the world shaming the strong (1 Corinthians 1:27). I have had a clearer view of the state that my heart really is in and whilst it often shocks and offends me, it is closer to the real me than the image of myself that I like to believe.

I am still walking with an emotional 'limp' and I hope that it remains if it gifts me with a clearer view of eternity and a way of sifting through life's upsets. Joy is always there if we seek it, although happiness may be something not worth searching for. I must learn to be content and be joyful at times when happiness eludes me.

Time has passed once more and the new member of our family has arrived. William was welcomed into the household with such joy. Again, I praised God, yet again it was bittersweet. Someone asked me when I was pregnant whether this baby was going to heal me. They were fairly far off the mark. William is a God-given distraction to my grief but he is not here to heal me, he is here to be loved and cherished. There will always be a Natalie-shaped hole in my heart and it cannot be filled by anyone else. My heart is now busy loving Will and my other precious children, and right now that is the task God has entrusted to me so I must set about doing it with all my might and his strength.

As my life continues to unfold I've had cause to ask myself some hard questions. Did I want to live life without her? No. Did I want to learn these painful lessons? Not intentionally; and yet through having empty arms that feel so bereft without her, God is filling our hearts. Our arms are empty yet his arms in heaven are full. We continue to struggle here, but her path of struggle is ended. Her life is complete. Nattie's eternity is with God and she is wonderfully, perfectly alive. Our hearts are aching, whilst her heart is full of praise for the God who made her, loves her and with whom she is now. God has taught us incredible truths about himself, eternity, heaven and my own frailty. Yet, like David I can say, 'I *will* praise Him' (Psalm 28:7).

I have learned in a small way all of the lessons in this book and yet I have not learned them completely.

I will not always remember them, I will get things out of perspective and I will forget to thank God for all that he has given me. I need reminding, I need rebuking and I need encouraging. So do you. If I have encouraged just one person to raise their heart towards heaven and thank God for something, then this book has been worth writing. I can't pretend to be a good example of a Christian, nor can I begin to put myself forward as an expert in suffering. I am only me, and a flawed one at that. The journey so far has often been painful; yet hard times are still to come. However, I am so thankful that my life is not pointless and I continue on this road with God as my Guide.

I do not know what will happen tomorrow, but he does; and if I have learnt anything throughout this, it is that he is completely trustworthy, utterly dependable, entirely faithful and an all-encompassing Comforter. When everything seemed to be at an end, he was still there. When my tears seemed to run out, he had stored them all for me (Psalm 56:8). When I felt that I was devoid of hope, his Word showed me that hope was all around me and he continues to comfort me on every side (Psalm 71:21).

So we continue our struggle, knowing that our lives are richer from having known and loved Natalie, and we are assured that whatever happens in the future, our merciful, awesome God will *always* work all things together for the good of those who love him (Romans 8:28).

O Natalie, Natalie the finality
Here on earth, that you went home
So soon.
We wanted you to stay longer
To share our journey.
We tried to protect you from harm, danger,
Difficulties,
But it came with stealth
Like a thief in the night
And took you home so suddenly, unexpectedly.
We were not ready.
How we loved you!
We saw your shell,
Your beautiful pale, silent, soft shell
And knew it was not you
And knew you were not there

The journey continues

And knew that you'd gone home.
Yet we are raging, riven with grief
Wanting the life to return,
Wanting you to come back and join us.
So we carry on incomplete
Trusting our Guide on the journey
Who tells us He has gone before;
That you've gone to softer scenes,
That you've gone to gentler, greener glades.
We have you in our hearts
We have our memories
We have you in our mind's eye
Constantly.
We see the reminders of you all around
And we are comforted
To have spent the time we did
To love you as we did.

Judy Grayburn 2006

13.
Helping others with empty arms

I am completely convinced that we could not have functioned as well as we did during those early days were it not for an amazing team of friends and family who initially rallied around us. It is hard to describe how a 'smog' of emotion descends upon you. You begin to function at such a basic level, that any practical tasks being done for you make a supreme difference to your ability to cope. We were so blessed to have had an almost military-inspired rota system that organized our ironing, washing, cleaning, cooking and shopping beautifully. People from all parts of the church helped out and God used their different abilities to comfort and bless us. People readily acknowledged that they might not have cooked very well but they could do cleaning, stain removal — you name it, they did it. We saw, and were humbled by, the willingness of others to stand with us and be immensely practical. From the shopping bags that arrived to someone offering freezer space, God interweaved people's gifts, time and willingness to create a system that the best social services department could not have rivalled. There were some really helpful things that people did and said, and I wanted to outline them in the hope that it might help others to feel more comfortable when helping during bereavement.

Be practical

For some, the thought of cleaning another person's bathroom is one step too far, but perhaps you could take round some basic food supplies. People really thought about what I liked and tried to tailor their thoughts accordingly. One couple brought round a scrapbook ready for me to begin compiling photographs. They knew just what I enjoyed doing and I so appreciated the fact that they had really considered me and brought a gift to encourage me to do something creative.

Here is a list of some more practical ideas that people had, which so helped us and may inspire you.

- Buying a rose bush for us in honour of Natalie.

- Planting something in their own garden and inviting us to go and see it.

- One lady preparing lunch boxes for our children so we didn't have to think about it.

- Offering lifts to places we needed to go to and accompanying Steve to difficult appointments.

- Making all the orders of service — and doing them so beautifully. I'd never have had the time.

- Sending books they thought would be comforting or useful.

- Amusing our children, helping them to keep smiling.

- Sending financial gifts to help with all the extra funeral expenses.

- Arranging all the food for the funeral.

- Printing off photographs they had of Nattie or putting them onto a CD-Rom for us.

- Taking me out to lunch with other friends.

- Having a day out arranged for me a couple of months later.

- Ringing me regularly to see how I was.

- Putting my bins out every 'bin day'.

- Placing flowers at her grave during the weeks following, when they knew I was so busy.

- Sending wonderful cards just to let me know that they were still praying for us or thinking about us.

- Encouraging me by talking about opportunities they had had to speak with other people about the Lord because of Natalie's death.

Be available

Helping others is about being available. Sometimes the best thing you can do is just to be there. We really need to just talk sometimes and finding someone happy to listen is not always easy. I had genuine offers of people being there for me during the night. I took them up on it twice, even though I didn't really want to bother them. I was so glad that they were there for me when I really needed them. Being able to chat about how you are feeling and share memories with them is so important in your healing process.

Be faithful

When you're grieving, your tolerance and patience levels are far lower than they were before you lost someone. You tend to 'hold' people to things in a much more stringent way and feel much more discouraged when people don't follow through. If you tell someone you'll do something, try if at all possible to keep your word. We're easily hurt and when everything else has fallen apart, we need reassurance that people are still faithful. Remembering significant dates is a really practical way of comforting people. There were some people who thought about us at particular times and told me they were thinking and praying for us. That meant an incredible amount to us.

Be prepared to cry

It might sound odd, but tears are very precious. They're significant enough for God to store them up (Psalm 56:8) and for the Bible to record that Jesus wept (John 11:35). When we went to the hospital the day that Natalie died, some of the staff cried. We were immensely touched by their tears. They were apologetic for their emotion but I told them that their tears were special to us because it meant that Natalie had touched them somehow. Other friends and acquaintances came round to our house to visit us. There were many tears; some were theirs, many were ours. Time and time again they apologized and said they had come to comfort us and not to fall apart. They didn't realize that their tears were far more of a comfort than some impersonal platitudes. There were many who were uncomfortable with my tears. Why do we find it so embarrassing? If you sit with someone, try and swallow your discomfort and simply let them cry. They will be really grateful. Sometimes just staying quiet, offering a tissue, a gentle touch or a hug will mean so much. We don't want to be told to be brave, or have someone try to short circuit our emotions. We have to cry; and tears are incredibly healing. My best comforters have often said very little; you can see comfort in their face. Their expression showed sympathy, shared pain and warmth. That was often all I needed; just to show me that they cared. You might not be the 'huggy' type but I would rather have had one hug than 1000 well-meaning words.

I know that some people were uncomfortable and that it was very hard for many even to come to our home. The fact that people had pushed themselves beyond their comfort zone to come and stand with us in grief is something that I'll never forget. Many said,

'I'm sorry, I don't know what to say.' That was fine! There really wasn't much to say. Just to hear 'I'm sorry' meant a lot to us. There were no obvious reasons for her death that we understood and having people trying to explain it away was rarely helpful and often hurtful. Often no words were more assuring than many. Never dismiss the power of human touch. Simple gestures convey a world of meaning and may be remembered long after words have been forgotten.

Be honest

When your feelings and life are laid bare for all to inspect, others' transparency is comforting. The fact that other people were honest about their feelings and their struggles was really helpful. We particularly valued insights from others who had been through bereavement before. Theological explanations were not what we really needed initially — they were maybe for a later date. We had already been struggling to come to terms with God's sovereignty but we found it patronizing coming from others. Words need to be chosen carefully when dealing with people who have raw emotions. We now laugh about some of the comments we received, but at the time, some folks completely stunned us. I'm not claiming that I've never done the same, but I learned from others that engaging your brain before opening your mouth is really wise! Bereaved people will appreciate hearing that you are finding it hard too. But be honest, don't claim to understand and try to be sensitive.

Be spiritual

When talking with bereaved people, a short prayer whether over the telephone or in person is really appreciated. People first asked us whether we minded, which was thoughtful. Praying with others was lovely; they often echoed our hearts' cries in ways that we weren't always able to express. A few people read the Bible with us. I think that unless you are visiting in an official capacity, you do need a good level of friendship first in order not to seem overbearing. One man came to see us and simply said, 'Do you know what I've been really blessed by this week?' He shared what he had learned from reading his Bible and we were really uplifted by the time that he had left. He wasn't linking it to our situation, we just had a chance to reflect on some encouragements from God's Word. He was more of a blessing than he'll ever realize. Another friend came and we just talked about heaven. We both cried, laughed, we shared our thoughts, prayed and my heart was strengthened. I am so thankful to God for people who were sensitively spiritual.

I hope that this has given you a little insight as to what might be helpful. Despite everything I've said, I would rather have seen people than not, no matter what they said or did. People have since asked me what to do or say with people who are bereaved and my advice is quite simple. Just show them that you care, ask them how they are doing today and be prepared to do something practical for them. God's hands are our hands here on earth and if we can embrace, help and love others, we are showing them our care and God's love too.

Postscript

Readers can learn more about God's love for little children by reading the Gospels (Matthew, Mark, Luke and John) and seeing how kindly and tenderly Jesus dealt with those very young in years — for example, in Mark 10:13-16 and Luke 18:15-17.

A list of further helpful books on the subject of bereavement can be found on a dedicated web site at www.emptyarmswithhope.co.uk

If you have found this book helpful or have any further questions, e-mail: emptyarms@epbooks.org

A wide range of Christian books is available from EP Books. If you would like a free catalogue please write to us or contact us by e-mail. Alternatively, you can view the whole catalogue online at our web site:

www.epbooks.org

EP BOOKS
Faverdale North, Darlington, DL3 0PH, England
e-mail: sales@epbooks.org

EP BOOKS USA
P. O. Box 614, Carlisle, PA 17013, USA
e-mail: usa.sales@epbooks.org